FARMERS
& FIGHTERS

JANE SHUTER

Heinemann
LIBRARY

First published in Great Britain by Heinemann Library
Halley Court, Jordan Hill, Oxford OX2 8EJ
a division of Reed Educational and Professional Publishing Ltd.
Heinemann is a registered trademark of Reed Educational & Professional Publishing Limited.

OXFORD MELBOURNE AUCKLAND KUALA LUMPUR
SINGAPORE IBADAN NAIROBI KAMPALA JOHANNESBURG
GABORONE PORTSMOUTH NH CHICAGO

Designed by Celia Floyd
Illustrations by Jeff Edwards and Donald Harley
Printed in Hong Kong by Wing King Tong Co., Ltd.

03 02 01 00 99
10 9 8 7 6 5 4 3 2 1

ISBN 0 431 00499 4
This title is also available in a hardback library edition (ISBN 0 431 00498 6).

British Library Cataloguing in Publication Data

Shuter, Jane
    Greece : farmers and fighters. - (Ancient world topic books)
    1 . Agriculture - Greece - History - Juvenile literature
    2 . Military Art and Science - Greece - History - Juvenile literature
    3 . Greece - History - To 146 B. C. - Juvenile literature
    I . Title
    938

Acknowledgements
The Publishers would like to thank the following for permission to reproduce photographs:
Ancient Art and Architecture Collection pp5, 21; Antiken-sammlungen, Munich p16; Art Institute of Chicago p25; Ashmolean Museum p8; Bildarchiv Preussischer Kulturbesitz p15; British Museum pp20, 23, 29; C M Dixon pp9, 17; Wadsworth Atheneum p7.

Cover photograph reproduced with permission of Bildarchiv Preussischer Kulturbesitz

Every effort has been made to contact copyright holders of any material reproduced in this book. Any omissions will be rectified in subsequent printings if notice is given to the Publisher.

Any words appearing in the text in bold, **like this**, are explained in the Glossary.

CONTENTS

INTRODUCTION

PERSIA

A e g e a n S e a

•Marathon
•Athens
Salamis

Sparta

M e d i t e r r a n e a n S e a

0		100 miles	
0		200 km	

MOUNTAINS AND SEA

Greece is a country that is broken up by mountains and the sea. In ancient times it was hard to get from one place to another. It was a long time before the Greeks thought of themselves as part of one country, even though they spoke the same language and had the same religion.

Timeline

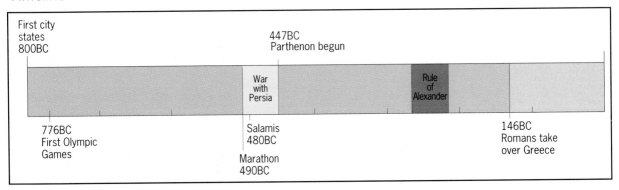

First city states 800BC

447BC Parthenon begun

War with Persia

Rule of Alexander

776BC First Olympic Games

Salamis 480BC

Marathon 490BC

146BC Romans take over Greece

CITY STATES

If people did not see themselves as Greek, what were they? Most people were part of a **city state** – a city and the land around it – and most were farmers. City states were small, some only had a few thousand families. Athens and Sparta were the biggest and most important city states.

Different city states were run in different ways. Some had one **ruler**, usually a king. Some were run by the most important men. Some were run by most of the free men of the city – the men who were not **slaves**. All city states expected the men to fight when there was a war. This book looks at two main occupations for men in Ancient Greece – fighting and farming.

The mountains of Greece were dry as well as steep. This meant that it was very hard to grow crops there.

Most men in a **city state** were expected to fight when there was a war. Women did not fight, nor did the sick or disabled. The soldiers had to bring their own weapons. **Archaeologists** have found remains on Greek battlefields. They show that some soldiers were in their teens and others were well over fifty years old.

PART-TIME FIGHTERS?

Sparta was the only city state with a full-time army. Every other army had soldiers who were also farmers. They could not fight all year round. They had to be at home at busy times of the farming year, such as harvest time. Spartan soldiers had sayings like: 'Come back with your shield or on it'. This meant they should either win (losers threw their shields away and ran) or die (the dead were carried home using their shields as stretchers). Part-time soldiers had a different view of the matter, as this poem shows:

A perfect shield is worn by some Thracian now.
I had no choice; I left it in a wood.
Oh well, I saved my skin, so let it go!
A new one's just as good.

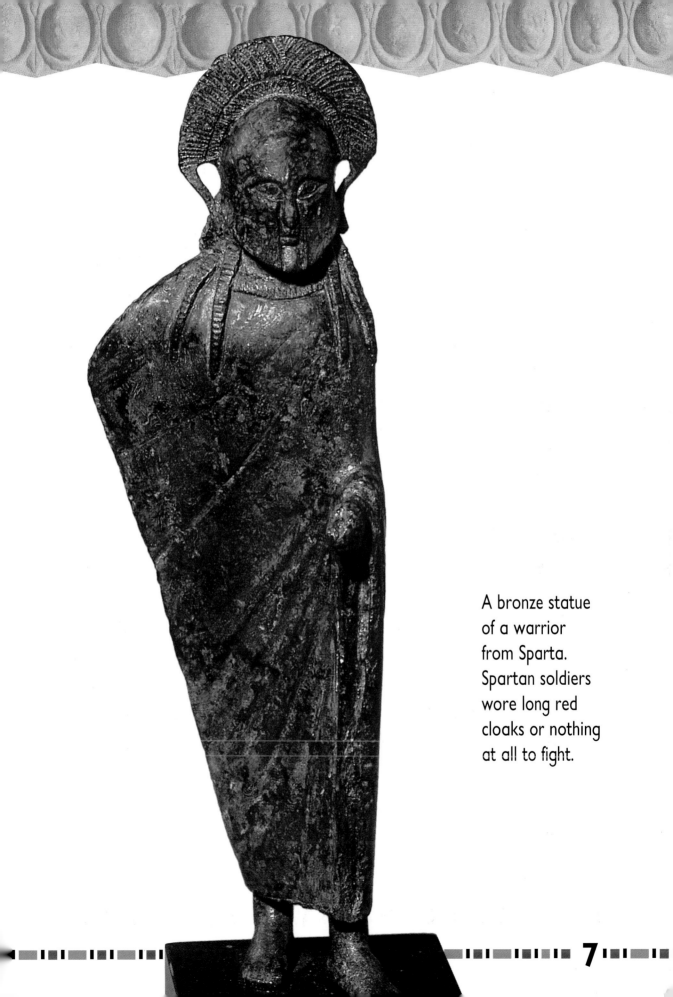

A bronze statue
of a warrior
from Sparta.
Spartan soldiers
wore long red
cloaks or nothing
at all to fight.

War was part of Greek life. Most Greek men expected to go to war regularly in their lifetimes, just as they expected to marry and have children. **City states** often fought each other. Sometimes they **traded** with each other and joined together to fight another city state. Small city states that were close to Athens or Sparta usually agreed to join them. They would probably have been forced to anyway. A small city state would see an advantage in joining a bigger one because the bigger one would protect it.

If another country invaded Greece, many city states might fight together. But, once the enemy was beaten, they soon started to fight each other again.

Greek boys playing with toy chariots. Children's fighting games made it easier for them to train for real war later.

This archer is part of the wall decoration from a Persian temple showing all kinds of Persian soldiers. The Persian army fought and dressed very differently from Greeks.

THE PERSIANS

Persia was Greece's nearest and most powerful neighbour. The Persians were a constant threat, even when they were not invading. They invaded Greece in 490BC (under King Darius) and in 480BC (under Darius' son, Xerxes). Both times the Greeks beat them back.

Greek land battles were fought mainly by **hoplites,** who fought standing shoulder to shoulder so their shields made a wall against the enemy attack. There were about six rows of soldiers. Those at the back pushed the rest forward. If a soldier fell, another one stepped from behind into the gap. If the wall of shields broke, the soldiers were easily killed and the battle was lost.

MARATHON, 490BC

In 490BC a huge Persian army landed at Marathon, about 40 kilometres from Athens. It had about 20,000 **archers**, men with spears and horsemen. Athens and the small **city state** of Plataea had just 10,000 men. Sparta promised help, but had to finish several days of **religious ceremonies** first.

By the time they arrived it was all over. First, both armies just watched each other for several days. Then, the Athenians made a surprise attack. The battle was long and hard, but the Athenians won. About 6400 Persians and 192 Greeks were killed. The dead were buried under a mound that is still there today. For years the Athenians were angry with the Spartans for not coming at once.

The battle of Marathon.

At first the Greeks fought at sea by getting close enough to the enemy ships for their soldiers to fight. But they soon found that sea battles could be won more easily by **ramming** enemy ships. The Greeks soon had several sorts of ships in sea battles. There were small, fast ships to take messages and big, heavy ships to ram. The heavy ships (triremes) had as many as 170 men rowing them. With lots of rowers the ships went faster and rammed harder.

SALAMIS, 480BC

In 480BC the Persians invaded and took over parts of Greece. They beat the Spartans at Thermopylae and marched on to Athens. About 400 Persian ships also sailed to Salamis, off the coast of Athens. About 300 Greek ships were waiting. They trapped the Persian attackers in a narrow channel, drawing up to make a line right across it. A Greek playwright described a Persian view of the battle:

The Greek ships were in a circle around us. They closed in and rammed. Our ships turned over; the sea was choked with wrecks and slaughtered men. The beaches and low rocks were covered in corpses.

The battle of Salamis

Because the Ancient Greeks fought so often, their doctors had a lot of practice in treating **wounds**. Even in the earliest battles, there were doctors on the battlefield. There was often one soldier in every group who was good at looking after wounds. They tried to clean the wounds, often with wine, which stops **infections**. They also gave herbs in wine to the wounded to make them sleepy and soothe the pain. They used the same herbs in ointments, too, for the same reasons.

In about 760BC a Greek writer, Homer, wrote long stories about adventures and battles. He also mentions, in passing, battlefield doctors:

Agamemnon commanded the doctor be brought to Menelaos, who was wounded by an **archer**. The arrow was still in his wound. When he came to where Menelaos was wounded he took out the arrow. But the pointed sides broke off in the wound as he did so. He skilfully sucked them out and then put on a soothing ointment that he carried with him.

This decoration from the bottom of a Greek drinking cup shows a soldier bandaging a friend's wounded arm. The arrow he has pulled out of the wound is by the injured man's knee.

EVIDENCE FROM THE TIME

We know about the **armour** Ancient Greeks wore and the weapons they used, because some remains have survived from the time. There are also vase paintings that show soldiers. Writings from the time also tell us about the armour they wore and how they fought.

IN ABOUT 760BC THE GREEK WRITER HOMER WROTE ABOUT HOW BATTLES WERE FOUGHT:

At last the armies met, with a clash of shields, spears and bronze-covered fighting men. The **bosses** of their shields collided and a great roar went up.

A vase painting of a hoplite. He is putting on his armour.

NEW EVIDENCE

Each time **archaeologists** excavate a battlefield they find armour from the time that they can study.

A Spartan buried on a recently excavated battlefield had an iron spear point still in his chest. This shows that if a spear was pushed hard enough it could go through the bronze chest-armour that **hoplites** wore.

Some hoplite armour – a helmet and chest armour. When it was being used it would have been polished until it shone.

The land in Greece is hard to farm, even today. A lot of it is too dry and hilly to grow much more than olive trees and **vines**. Ancient Greek paintings show farmers growing **crops** with very simple wooden tools.

THE FARMING YEAR

The farmers ploughed the fields and sowed the seeds in October, just before the rain that would help the seeds to grow. The **grain** was harvested in May. In September they harvested olives and grapes, which they made into oil and wine. They also grew other fruit, beans and vegetables that were ready in September.

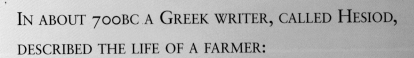

IN ABOUT 700BC A GREEK WRITER, CALLED HESIOD, DESCRIBED THE LIFE OF A FARMER:

There will be no rest ever from toil and hardship during the day, nor from suffering at night. You must work to avoid **famine** and earn the love of the corn goddess, who will fill your barns. After the harvest there may be time to rest in the shade of a rock with wine and goat's cheese.

Farmland in city states was all around the city.

Farmers grew **grain**, fruit and vegetables on the flat land around the cities. Greece did not have much land that was good for growing **crops**, so **city states** often found it hard to grow enough food for everyone. This was especially true of the big city states, such as Athens. City states often had to **trade** the **goods** they made a lot of (like oil and wine) for food from other countries, such as Egypt.

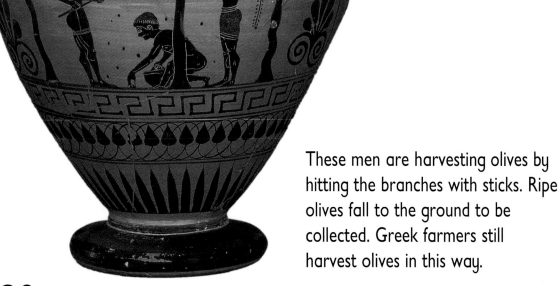

These men are harvesting olives by hitting the branches with sticks. Ripe olives fall to the ground to be collected. Greek farmers still harvest olives in this way.

MOVING ON

Between 700 and 500BC, many groups of Greeks moved to live and do their farming in other places. There just was not enough land in Greece for them all to farm. The first of these **colonies** was in Italy. Then the Greeks set up colonies all along the Mediterranean coast and around the Black Sea. People in these colonies kept their Greek ways. They traded some of the food they grew with Greece, usually with the city state they had left.

A pottery model of some women making bread, a very important food. Most city states had to buy grain from other countries so that everyone would have bread all year round.

KEEPING ANIMALS

Cattle were used to pull **ploughs**. Goats were kept mostly for milk and cheese; sheep for wool which was spun into thread. Animal skins were made into leather for shoes and clothes. Chickens were kept for eggs, and were eaten when they stopped laying. Bees in hives made honey to sweeten food and drink.

MEAT

The Greeks did not eat a lot of meat. They sometimes ate chicken or goat. They ate meat mostly after **religious festivals**, when animals were **sacrificed**, then eaten afterwards.

THE GREEK WRITER HOMER DESCRIBES A SACRIFICE BEFORE A BATTLE:

When they had prayed and scattered grain they slit the throat of an ox for sacrifice. They skinned it, burned the thighs and entrails as a sacrifice. They cut the rest into small pieces, put them on sticks stripped of leaves and roasted them over a fire. Then they ate the meat, sharing it equally between them.

The Greeks often hunted wild
animals, for fun and for the meat.

ALL KINDS OF FISH

In Ancient Greek times the seas and rivers of Greece were full of fish. The Greeks ate a lot of fish. Fish was not often given as a **sacrifice** like red meat. Instead, it was eaten as part of ordinary meals almost every day. The Greeks ate fish, squid, octopus and shellfish. They roasted them, grilled them and baked them with sauces. They ate them hot or cold.

CATCHING FISH

Ancient Greek paintings show fishermen catching fish in nets from boats, and lobsters in cages made from twigs. People also fished with a fishing line and a pole.

TRICKING CUSTOMERS

People in the cities bought fish from the market. The fish was brought in early in the morning from fishing villages along the coast. Plays from the time talk about fish-sellers in markets pouring water over their fish to make it seem fresher than it really was!

ONE OF THE EARLIEST COOKERY RECIPES EVER WRITTEN DOWN IS A GREEK RECIPE FROM ABOUT 400BC. IT IS A RECIPE FOR COOKING FISH:

Cut off the head of the ribbon fish. Wash it carefully and cut it into slices. Pour cheese and oil over it. Bake it.

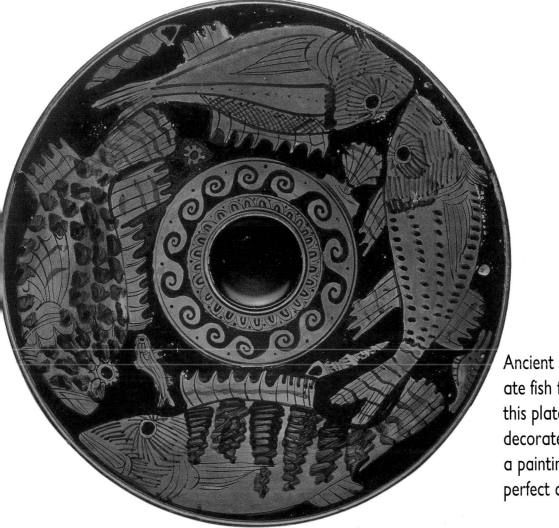

Ancient Greeks ate fish from this plate. It is decorated with a painting of the perfect catch!

STORING

Wine, water and oil were stored in large pottery jars. Many of these have survived. Fish was dried or preserved in oil in jars or bottles. **Grain** was bought and **ground** into flour for bread nearly every day. It was stored in bins in barns on farms.

COOKING

The Greeks cooked food over an open fire or in the oven. Ovens were mostly used for bread. Most cooking, roasting, grilling and boiling or baking in pots was done on metal grills over an open fire. This could be done inside or outside, depending on the weather. Ordinary people probably had a cooking **hearth** outside and in a corner of their main room. Bigger houses had a kitchen.

Cooking in an Athenian town house.

ORDINARY MEALS

Breakfast was usually just bread and cheese or fruit. This was the midday meal too, perhaps with some fish or vegetables left over from dinner the day before. The main meal of the day was eaten in the evening. People ate fish, vegetables and bread. Ordinary people did not eat meat except at **religious ceremonies**, unless they caught a wild animal. Richer people might eat some meat, such as sausages, chicken or small wild birds. They only ate lamb, pork, beef or goat at **feasts** or religious ceremonies.

DINNER PARTIES

Men often had dinner parties, which women and children could not go to. The servants cleared up while the guests sat and drank wine. They ate and drank lying on couches. Women entertainers danced and played music for them.

A male dinner party. The men took off their shoes and lay on couches while they were entertained by musicians and dancers.

archaeologists people who dig up and study things left behind from past times

archer a soldier who fights with a bow and arrows

armour coverings for different parts of the body to protect soldiers in battles. Armour is usually made of metal

bosses protective metal piece in the centre of a shield

cattle cows and bulls

city state a city and the land it controls around it

colonies places set up in one country by people from another country

crops plants that farmers grow for food or to use in other ways (to make clothes, baskets or paper)

famine a time when there is not enough food and people die of hunger

feast a special meal with lots of different things to eat and drink. Feasts often celebrate special days.

goods things that are made, bought and sold

grain types of grasses with fat seeds which are eaten. Barley, wheat, rye, oats and rice are all grains.

ground crushing grain up until the seeds are a powder (flour)

hearth a flat bed of stones for lighting a fire on

hoplites soldiers who fought on foot, with spears

infection something which gets into wounds and makes the patient sick

plough a tool that turns over the soil to break it up

ramming sailing straight at another ship and running into it to try to sink it

religious ceremonies special times when people go to one place to pray to a god or goddess

ruler the person who runs the country

sacrifices something given to a god or goddess as a gift. If the sacrifice was a living thing it was killed before it was given.

slaves people who are treated by their owners as property. They can be bought and sold and are not free to leave.

trade this has two meanings:
  1 a job, for example 'shoemaking is his trade'
  2 selling or swapping goods, for example 'Greece traded oil for grain'

vines the plants that grapes grow on

wounds injuries

INDEX